AF887059

The Power of a Promise

finding the power to be your best.

Todd Duncan

Student Workbook

Note: Please do not duplicate any of this material. Additional copies may be purchased at your local bookstore or through www.thomasnelson.com.

WELCOME LETTER FROM TODD DUNCAN

Dear friend,

We are getting ready to embark on an exciting journey together.

Over the past few years, I've been able to walk through periods of life with people just like you who are being challenged to grow to a deeper level of commitment in their relationship and others.

As you grow in your ability to make and keep promises, you will find that your integrity, self worth and level of respect with others will increase significantly. I'm so glad that we get to take this journey together.

You are going to grow over the next four weeks — get ready!

Your friend,

Todd Duncan
www.theduncangroup.com

TABLE OF CONTENTS

INTRODUCTION

It is a trap for a man to dedicate to something rashly and only later to consider his vows.
— King Solomon, Proverbs 20:25, NIV

Welcome to *The Power of A Promise*. This course was designed to teach you how to do one thing: close the gap between what is promised and what is performed in your life. A lot of people feel the sting of living a life that is less than what they had expected — we don't want you to be among them!

As you learn to keep promises to yourself, you will see the power that these right decisions have on your life — and the impact that you will begin to have on those closest to you.

Over the next few weeks, we are going to cover the power of promise making in four critical areas:

- Personal Promises
- Professional Promises
- Partner Promises
- Prayerful Promises

You will see the power of a changed life over the next few weeks — your own.

INTRODUCTION TO *THE POWER OF A PROMISE*

Lesson thesis

Too often there is a gap between what is promised and what is performed; yet the platform for personal and professional success, satisfaction and significance is always built not on the promises you make but on the promises you keep.

Ask yourself...

If 60 Minutes secretly followed you for a week of video taping, would they find that you are ...

- Keeping your commitments to your spouse and children?
- Spending your money how you intend?
- Honoring your word to your co-workers?
- Maintaining your body as you'd like?
- Meeting your professional goals?
- Adhering to your spiritual standards?

To close the gap between what you promise and what you perform ... take these three steps first:

1. ______________________________.
   Promises should always be in tune with your life-purpose. That purpose is the ____________ through which all your ____________ are made and from which your ____________ is ____________.

2. ______________________________.
   Promises should always compliment not contradict your core values. Do you know yours? When was the last time you spent an hour thinking?

   You cannot promise what you are not committed to personally.

   A simple man believes anything, but a prudent man gives thought to his steps.
   — King Solomon, Proverbs 14:15, NIV

3. ______________________________.
   You must know where you're going before you can truly commit to action.

LESSON ONE: THE POWER OF PERSONAL PROMISES

As you go and grow throughout life, you should always be looking at where you are and toward where you want to go. That creative tension is good because it ushers in a series of "promise making" to yourself and to others. How you articulate and keep your promises will be the unalterable keystone for every success you will enjoy for the rest of your life. Conversely, not to keep your promises will have its own unsavory effect.... As you continue to change, transition and move closer to the person you want to be, you will need to focus on what I call the really big question: ***If my life were perfect, how would it be different?*** *Ponder this question because it has within it the guidance system that can help direct you to making promises that lead to a life of joy and fulfillment.*
— Todd Duncan, *The Power to Be Your Best,* pgs. 234-235

Personal Promises
Promises you make to you

You must first ______________________________ promises to yourself before you qualify to ______________________________ promises to others.

Ask yourself …

- How do I want to be remembered?
- What matters most to me?
- What must I do today to secure a successful and satisfying tomorrow?

Keys to making and keeping personal promises:

1. Decide to order your life based on a sense of ______________________.
2. Decide: What are your priorities and do you have a sense of order about those priorities?
3. Decide what you could do today that would make you feel better about ______________________.

Three Personal Promises You Should Keep

1. Promise to live with ____________________.

- It's the foundation of self-worth
  I desire so to conduct the affairs of this administration that if at the end, when I come to lay down the reins of power, I have lost every other friend on earth, I shall at least have one friend left, and that friend shall be down inside of me.
  — Abraham Lincoln

- It's the cornerstone of true success

2. Promise to never stop ______________________________, ______________________________ and ______________________________.

■ Don't fear failure; learn from it — "fail forward."

He who makes no mistakes makes no progress.
— Teddy Roosevelt

The person who is incapable of making a mistake is incapable of anything.
— Abraham Lincoln

■ The secret to your success lies in your daily routine. Master the daily disciplines and you will master your life.

We can never become what we need to be by remaining what we are.
— Max Dupree, *Leadership is an Art*

Schedule your priorities, don't prioritize your schedule.
— Dr. Stephen Covey

3. Promise to __________________-________________________ to others.

■ Give more than you receive.

■ Give on a ratio of 4:1.

It is in giving that we receive.
— St. Francis of Assisi

Results of personal promise making

People who feel good about themselves produce good results.
— Ken Blanchard and Spencer Johnson in *The One-Minute Manager*

1. Create success

2. Offer satisfaction

A person may possess many practical skills and be able to apply them well yet have a very low self-esteem. This person may feel a great discomfort at the thought of having to learn a new skill or change his environment in any meaningful way. Another person with a high self-esteem may be lacking in practical skills but have no fear of learning or of confronting a new environment and can quickly and enjoyably learn and adapt to different situations. In the latter example, the person had confidence in his or her ability — based on a healthy self-esteem. Self-leadership is a mandate in the area of personal promises.

Action Steps I Will Take This Week...

Answer Key: Pursue your purpose, filter, decisions, motivation, maximized, Validate your values, Verify your vision, keep, make, balance, you, integrity, learning, stretching, growing, add-value

NOTES

LESSON TWO: THE POWER OF PROFESSIONAL PROMISES

The integrity of the upright guides them, but the unfaithful are destroyed by their duplicity.
— King Solomon, Proverbs 11:3, NIV

Review:
Personal Promises
- Promise to live with integrity
- Promise to never stop learning, stretching and growing
- Promise to add value to others

THE SECOND AREA IN WHICH YOU MUST KEEP YOUR PROMISES ...

Professional Promises
Promises you make regarding your career

Ask yourself ...

- Can I always be trusted to follow through with my word on the job?
- Do I recognize the value of and need for teamwork in professional success?
- Am I making a living or making a life?

Keys to making and keeping professional promises:

1. Integrity

2. Teamwork

3. Significance

Three Professional Promises You Should Keep

1. Promise to value ______________________ over ______________________.

- You make a living by what you get, you make a life by what you give.

It's easy to make a buck. It's a lot harder to make a difference.
— Tom Brokaw

You can have everything you want in life if you just help enough other people get what they want.
— Zig Ziglar

- Never invest more in possessions than people.

Money is like muck, not good unless it be spread.
— Francis Bacon

2. Promise to value ____ over convention and ____ over institution.

- Every person is only one idea away from greater success.

Nothing is more dangerous than an idea when it is the only one we have.
— Alain

- It takes innovation to get on top and more innovation to stay there.

Allow me to furnish the interior of my head as I please, and I shall put up with a hat like everybody else's.
— Henri Bergson

3. Promise to value ______________________________ over problems, policies or positions.

- People are your greatest professional asset.

Take away my people but leave my factories and soon grass will grow on the factory floor. Take away my factories but leave my people and soon we will have a new and better factory.
— Andrew Carnegie

What makes a good manager? Someone asked Yogi Bera.
A good ball club, Yogi replied.

Application: Accountability and Professional Promises

As iron sharpens iron, so one man sharpens another.
— King Solomon, Proverbs 27:17, NIV

The Benefits of Having Accountability

In the area of professional promises, accountability is key.

1. You will make better **choices.**

The choices we make by accident are just as important as the choices we make by design. You cannot manage your life if you do not manage your self. You cannot manage yourself if you do not manage your choices. Manage your choices and you will manage your life.
— Shad Helmstetter

2. You will experience more **clarity.**

There arises from a bad and inapt formation of words and thoughts, a wonderful obstruction to the mind.
— Francis Bacon

3. You will have a stronger **commitment.**

There are countless ways of achieving greatness, but any road to achieving one's maximum potential must be built on the bedrock of self respect for the individual, a commitment to excellence, and a rejection of mediocrity.
— Buck Rogers

4. You will gain more **certainty.**

...Human beings are creatures of habit. But, the only difference between a rut and a grave is it's length, depth, and how long you are in it.
— Art Holst

5. You will have more **consistency.**

You are what you repeatedly do; excellence is therefore not an act, but a habit.
— Aristotle

6. You will possess more **credibility.**

What you get by reaching your destination isn't nearly as important as what you become by reaching that destination.
— Zig Ziglar

...Every exaggeration of the truth once detected by others destroys our credibility and makes all that we do and say suspect.
— Stephen Covey

To order *The Power to Be Your Best*, which Todd mentioned earlier, just call 800-933-9673 or order online at www.nelsonword.com.

Action Steps I Will Take This Week...

Answer Key: significance, salary, creativity, innovation, people

NOTES

LESSON THREE: THE POWER OF PARTNER PROMISES

We can do no great things — only small things with great love.
— Mother Theresa

Review:
Personal Promises
- Promise to live with integrity
- Promise to never stop learning, stretching and growing
- Promise to add value to others

Professional Promises
- Promise to value significance over salary
- Promise to value creativity over convention and innovation over institution
- Promise to value people over problems, policies or positions

THE THIRD AREA IN WHICH YOU MUST KEEP YOUR PROMISES ...

Partner Promises
Promises you make to your spouse, family and closest friends

Being busy can either add to or take away from our abundance. One of the downsides of busyness often takes the form of work. If we are not careful, we can be driven by our schedules or a desire for fame and fortune. We can become workaholics and feed our fast-paced existence until it is satisfied only when it can get a little more stimuli, and a little more adrenaline flowing. Millions of people are becoming successful, but could they be missing the bigger goal of attaining significance?

Keys to ordering the power of a partner promise

1. ____________________________________

2. ____________________________________

3. ____________________________________

Three Partner Promises You Should Keep

1. Promise to put your partners' ______________________ before your own.

■ Leave your ego at the door.

People wrapped up in themselves make very small packages.
— Anonymous

EGO: Edging God Out.
—Ken Blanchard

■ Be creative; have fun.

No sacrifice is worth the name unless it is a joy. Sacrifice and a long face go ill together.
— Mohandas K. Gandhi

2. Promise to ______________________________ ______________________________ to your partners' success and well-being.

■ Listen first, speak last, and only if necessary.

I will begin to speak, when I have that to say which had not better be unsaid.
— Cato the younger, replying to criticism for being silent

■ Invest your own resources in their goals.

A generous man will prosper; he who refreshes others will himself be refreshed.
— King Solomon, Proverbs 11:25, NIV

3. Promise to demonstrate your ___________________________ every chance you get.

Greater love has no man than this, that a man lay down his life for his friends.
— Jesus, John 15:13

■ Hold true to your commitments.

Marriage is a matter of commitment, not a matter of convenience.
— Todd Duncan

■ Give them your time

Remember, your family spells love: T-I-M-E.
— Zig Ziglar

Results of partner promises

1. ____________________________________

2. ____________________________________

Application:

Questions that are worth considering...

1. We are moving through life faster but the real question is, do we have more time?

2. Do the things that you have worked so hard for provide you with true contentment?

The two great lies in life

Lie #1: Someday life will settle down.

Lie #2: Having more is better.

Ask yourself ...

- Am I spending quality time with my family on a regular basis?
- Am I selfless with my time, energy and resources?
- Am I adding value without keeping score?
- Do my closest friends consider me trustworthy?

Action Steps I Will Take This Week...

Answer Key: servitude, selflessness, generosity, needs, actively contribute, love, trust, love

NOTES

LESSON FOUR: THE POWER OF PRAYERFUL PROMISES

The things, Good Lord, that I pray for, give me thy grace to labor for.
— Sir Thomas More

Spirituality is not a pious pose. It is not a "Thou shalt not"; it is "Thou shalt." It flings open the doors into the eternal blessedness, energies and resources of God. It is a serious thing to remove the element of relaxation and play from any life. We cannot be normal physically, mentally or spiritually if we neglect this vital factor in human life. God [alone] has provided that our joy shall be full."
— Lewis Sperry Chafer, *He That is Spiritual*

The prayer of a righteous man is powerful and effective.
— James 5:16, NIV

Review:

Personal Promises

- Promise to live with integrity
- Promise to never stop learning, stretching and growing
- Promise to add value to others

Professional Promises

- Promise to value significance over salary
- Promise to value creativity over convention and innovation over institution
- Promise to value people over problems, policies or positions

Partner Promises

- Promise to put your partner's needs before your own
- Promise to actively contribute to your partner's success and well-being
- Promise to demonstrate love every chance you get

THE FOURTH AREA IN WHICH YOU MUST KEEP YOUR PROMISES ...

Prayerful Promises
Promises you make to God

Four things happen when you make promises to God. You'll find:

1. Your ______________________________ is enhanced.

2. Your ______________________________ is reduced.

3. Your ______________________________ is enhanced.

4. And, you'll have a greater spirit of ______________________________.

Prayer completes us. It is the lifeline of the created to their Creator. Through prayer you come to be the person you were created to be.

Nothing is more important than the promises you keep to God. True success begins on your knees. True life is lived on your knees.

Three Prayerful Promises You Should Keep

1. Promise to be grateful in ______________________________.

- Being grateful ***in*** everything is different than being grateful ***for*** everything.

I have never wished there was a God to call on — I have often wished there was a God to thank.
— F. Scott Fitzgerald

Give thanks in all circumstances...
— The Apostle Paul, I Thessalonians 5:18, NIV

- God knows what He's doing.

And we know that in all things God works for the good of those who love him, who have been called according to his purpose.
— The Apostle Paul, Romans 8:28, NIV

2. Promise to ______________________________ before you ______________________________.

■ Solitude precedes and feeds spiritual fulfillment.

When God is the center of the soul, although disasters may crowd in on all sides and roar like the waves of the sea, there is a constant calm within. The world can neither give nor take away this kind of peace.
— Archbishop Leighton

Prayer is an invitation to God to intervene in our lives.
— Abraham Joshua Heschel, *Man's Quest for God*

Silence is deep as eternity; speech is shallow as time.
— Thomas Carlyle

Be still and know that I am God.
— Psalm 46:10, NIV

■ Listening must precede learning.

You have made known to me the path of life; you will fill me with joy in your presence, with eternal pleasures at your right hand.
— King David, Psalms 16:11, NIV

Call to me and I will answer you and tell you great and unsearchable things you do not know.
— Jeremiah 33:3, NIV

3. Promise to ______________________________ before you ______________________________.

■ To stay on track with your purpose, you must stay in tune with God.

We walk by faith and not by sight.
— The Apostle Paul, II Corinthians 5:7, NASB

Without faith it is impossible to please God...
— The Apostle Paul, Hebrews 11:6, NIV

■ God's advice should always be your first priority in your life.

But seek first his kingdom and his righteousness, and all these will be given to you as well.
— Jesus, Matthew 6:33, NIV

If you want to know God's will for your life, do the next thing he asks you to do.
— Oswald Chambers

Results of prayerful promises:

1. Improved spiritual ____________________________.
2. Increased ____________________________ with Him.
3. Larger ____________________________ in your life.
4. More inner __________________________ in your soul.

Come to me, all you who are weary and burdened, and I will give you rest. Take my yoke upon you and learn from me, for I am gentle and humble in heart, and you will find rest for you souls. For my yoke is easy and my burden is light.
— Jesus, Matthew 11:28, NIV

Application:

To enter that relationship with the Creator we must be open to speaking to God as a friend. Pastor, author and United States Senate Chaplain Lloyd John Olgilvie says it like this:

Nothing is more important. It is the source of life's greatest joy. There is no power or peace without it. With it, we receive supernatural insight and wisdom. Our ability to understand and love people is maximized. We think more clearly and can act more decisively. Our problems shrink and we can tackle opportunities with gusto. Most of all, we fulfill the reason we were born: to know and love God.
— Lloyd John Olgilvie, *Conversations with God*

As you prepare to pray, consider these suggestions:

1. Pray ____________________________.

   You can pray at any time, at any place, about anything. Prayer is your personal dialog with God.

2. Pray with ____________________________ and experience His purpose.

   God uses kingdom principles to accomplish his purpose. He reveals his ways to you because that is how He accomplishes his purpose for you.

3. Pray with ______________________________.

Realize that God loves you more than you can ever imagine. Love him back with your words, your energy and how you prioritize your life.

4. Pray for ______________________________.

God has said we are his most important creation. He tells us not to worry, for He will provide.

5. Pray for ______________________________.

There are great forces in our world that threaten us as. God will build a wall of protection from these evils around you if you will only ask.

6. Pray for ______________________________.

You know people who need the power of Almighty God in their lives. Bring these friends and associates to God in prayer.

7. Pray ______________________________.

The goal of prayer is to transport your joys and sorrows to God's level, not to bring God to the level of your life experience. His timing is always right and always best.

Conclusion

Commit to make and keep the kind of powerful promises that will not only positively change our lives and help us reach our potential, but also change the lives of others and help them reach their potential. And with each promise we keep, we will take one step closer to becoming the complete person we were created to be.

Action Steps I Will Take This Week...

Answer Key: character, vulnerability, faith, humility, everything, listen, speak, seek, step, purpose, intimacy, joy, peace, constantly, purpose, passion, provision, protection, people, patiently

NOTES

OTHER EZ LESSON PLANS

The EZ Lesson Plan was designed with the facilitator in mind. This new format gives you the flexibility as a teacher to use the video as the visual and then refer to the facilitator's guide for the questions … and even better, the answers. It is designed for a four-week study, communicated by our top authors and it is totally self-contained. **Each EZ Lesson Plan requires the student's guides to be purchased separately as we have maintained a very low purchase price on the video resource.**

Please visit your local Christian bookstore to see the other titles we have available in the EZ Lesson Plan format. We have listed some of the titles and authors for your convenience:

EZ LESSON PLANS NOW AVAILABLE:

The 10 Commandments of Dating

Ben Young and Dr. Samuel Adams

AVAILABLE NOW

Are you tired of pouring time, energy, and money into relationships that start off great and end with heartache? If so, you need The 10 Commandments of Dating to give you the hard-hitting, black-and-white, practical guidelines that will address your questions and frustrations about dating. This guide will help you keep your head in the search for the desire of your heart.

EZ Lesson Plan ISBN: 0-7852-9619-0 **Student's Guide ISBN: 0-7852-9621-2**

Extreme Evil: Kids Killing Kids

Bob Larson

AVAILABLE NOW

Kids are killing kids in public schools! Kids are killing their parents! What is causing all of this evil in our younger generation? Do we need prayer back in the schools … or do we need God to start in the home? Bob Larson gets us to the root of these evils and brings us some of the answers we are looking for in this new video assisted program.

EZ Lesson Plan ISBN: 0-7852-9701-4 **Student's Guide ISBN: 0-7852-9702-2**

Life Is Tough, but God Is Faithful

Sheila Walsh

AVAILABLE NOW

Sheila takes a look at eight crucial turning points that can help you rediscover God's love and forgiveness. Showing how the choices you make affect your life, she offers insights from the book of Job, from her own life, and from the lives of people whose simple but determined faith helped them become shining lights in a dark world.

EZ Lesson Plan ISBN: 0-7852-9618-2 **Student's Guide ISBN: 0-7852-9620-4**

Why I Believe

D. James Kennedy

AVAILABLE NOW

In this video, Dr. D. James Kennedy offers intelligent, informed responses to frequently heard objections to the Christian faith. By dealing with topics such as the Bible, Creation, the Resurrection and the return of Christ, Why I Believe provides a solid foundation for Christians to clarify their own thinking while becoming more articulate in the defense of their faith.

EZ Lesson Plan ISBN: 0-8499-8770-9 **Student's Guide ISBN: 0-8499-8769-5**

The Lord's Prayer

Jack Hayford

AVAILABLE NOW

Why do we say "Thy Kingdom come?" What does "Hallowed be Thy Name" mean? Do we really practice "Forgive us our debts as we forgive our debtors?" Pastor Jack Hayford walks you through verse-by-verse and then applies his great scripture to our personal lives. This study will put "meaning to the words" you have just been saying for years.

EZ Lesson Plan ISBN: 0-7852-9442-2 **Student's Guide ISBN: 0-7852-9609-3**

How To Pray

Ronnie Floyd

AVAILABLE NOW

Whether you are a rookie in prayer or a seasoned prayer warrior, this video kit will meet you where you are and take you to another level in your prayer life. You may have been raised in a Christian home where prayer was a normal, daily exercise. You may have attended church all of your life, where the prayers of the people and the minister were as common as the hymns that still ring in your ears. Yet such experiences do not guarantee that you know how to pray. With simple, yet profound prose, Dr. Floyd declares, "Prayer occurs when you depend on God, prayerlessness occurs when you depend on yourself."

EZ Lesson Plan ISBN: 0-8499-8790-3 **Student's Guide ISBN: 0-8499-8793-8**

Healing Prayer

Reginald Cherry, M.D.

AVAILABLE NOW

"Prayer is the divine key that unlocks God's pathway to healing in both the natural and supernatural realms of life." In Healing Prayer, he explores the connection between faith and healing, the Bible and medicine. Cherry blends the latest research, true stories, and biblical principles to show that spirit-directed prayers can bring healing for disease.

EZ Lesson Plan ISBN: 0-7852-9666-2 **Student's Guide ISBN: 0-7852-9667-0**

Jesus and The Terminator

Jack Hayford

AVAILABLE NOW

From the **E-Quake** Series comes the EZ Lesson Plan that is the focal point of the Book of Revelation. Pastor Hayford sets the stage for the fight against the Evil One when the end of time comes upon us. There is no greater force than that of Jesus and now viewers will see Him become triumphant again in this battle that is evident.

EZ Lesson Plan ISBN: 0-7852-9601-8 **Student's Guide ISBN: 0-7852-9658-1**

The Law of Process

John C. Maxwell

AVAILABLE NOW

Leadership develops daily, not in a day. This law, taken from **The Twenty One Irrefutable Laws of Leadership** is the first of the series to be placed into an individual study. Take each opportunity as it comes along and find the answer in a way only strong leaders would do it … by processing it. John explains how and why "Champions don't become champions in the ring … they are merely recognized there."

EZ Lesson Plan ISBN: 0-7852-9671-9 **Student's Guide ISBN: 0-7852-9672-7**

Forgiveness

John MacArthur

AVAILABLE NOW

In this three-session EZ Lesson Plan, noted biblical scholar John MacArthur provides an insightful look at forgiveness. MacArthur not only reminds us that we are called to grant forgiveness to those who sin against us, but he also teaches the importance of learning to accept the forgiveness of others.

EZ Lesson Plan ISBN: 0-8499-8808-X **Student's Guide ISBN: 0-8499-8809-8**

Created To Be God's Friend

Henry Blackaby

AVAILABLE NOW

Henry Blackaby being born a man of God, living his life as a man of God, teaches us how all of us are created equal in being God's friend. No Christian need live without a keen sense of purpose, and no believer need give up on finding daily closeness with God.

EZ Lesson Plan ISBN: 0-7852-9718-9 **Student's Guide ISBN: 0-7852-6758-1**

The Murder of Jesus

John MacArthur

AVAILABLE NOW

To many, the story of Christ's crucifixion has become so familiar that is has lost its ability to shock, outrage or stir any great emotion. In *The Murder of Jesus*, John MacArthur presents this pivotal moment in the life of Jesus in a way that forces the viewers to witness this event in all its power. The passion of Christ is examined chronologically through the lens of the New Testament with special attention given to Jesus' words on the cross, the miracles that attended the crucifixion, and the significance of Christ's atoning work.

EZ Lesson Plan ISBN: 0-8499-8796-2 **Student's Guide ISBN: 0-8499-8797-0**

Fresh Brewed Life

Nicole Johnson

AVAILABLE NOW

God is calling us to wake up, to shout an enthusiastic "Yes" to life, just as we say "Yes" to our first cup of coffee each morning. Nothing would please Him more than for us to live fresh-brewed lives steeped with His love, filling the world with the marvelous aroma of Christ. The EZ Lesson Plan will provide humor, vignettes, and in depth study to small groups all over on this topic.

EZ Lesson Plan ISBN: 0-7852-9723-5 **Student's Guide ISBN: 0-7852-9724-3**

The Law of Respect

John C. Maxwell

AVAILABLE NOW

We are taught from our parents to respect others. Our business practices are to be ones of respecting others ideas, thoughts and mainly their motivations. We tend to get caught up in the daily routines, but if we do not respect those around us and the ones we work with, our success will be held at a low ebb. John Maxwell is a leader's leader.

EZ Lesson Plan ISBN: 0-7852-9756-1 **Student's Guide ISBN: 0-7852-9757-X**

Becoming A Woman of Grace

Cynthia Heald

AVAILABLE NOW

This is a newly formatted product built around a message that only Cynthia Heald could deliver to us. Women have proven to be the stronger of the sexes in prayer, empathy and faith. Cynthia leads this women's group study on how a woman can become A Woman of Grace through prayer, obedience to God and other practices of their lives. This EZ Lesson Plan will bring the components of this publishing product to one, self-contained format ready to start small groups.

EZ Lesson Plan ISBN: 0-7852-9706-5 **Student's Guide ISBN: 0-7852-9707-3**

Avoiding Mr. Wrong

Stephen Arterburn

AVAILABLE NOW

If you are finding yourself attracted to the same type man over and over, there are several things you need to know before getting involved. Is the man Mr. Right or Mr. Wrong? Is he attractive to you for all the wrong reasons? *Avoiding Mr. Wrong* is more than just your checklist for the type of men to steer clear of. If you have already married Mr. Wrong do not fret, it's not too late. Understanding yourself and your spouse better is the first step to helping your Mr. Wrong become Mr. Right.

EZ Lesson Plan ISBN: 0-7852-9858-4 **Student's Guide ISBN: 0-7852-9859-2**

The Law of E.F. Hutton

John C. Maxwell

AVAILABLE NOW

The *Law of E.F. Hutton* is about gaining respect as a leader. When Alan Greenspan speaks before Congress, everybody listens. When he prepares to make a statement on lending rates, the entire financial community stops what it is doing. Billy Graham gets a similar kind of respect because of his unquestionable integrity and lifetime service. The Law of E.F. Hutton reveals itself in just about every situation. In this study, you will find how a real leader holds the power, not just the position.

EZ Lesson Plan ISBN: 0-7852-9806-1 **Student's Guide ISBN: 0-7852-9807-X**

Live God Loud

Ron Luce

AVAILABLE APRIL 24, 2001

In today's world, kids are drawn to an image. This might be a sports figure, a singer or even a brand of clothing. Finding an image is ok … unless it controls your mind and actions. Ron Luce, one of the top youth communicators, first wrote the book *Live God Loud* and now it is being made into an EZ Lesson Plan. This is the first youth product to be produced in this format. Most teens do not believe that living for God is "cool", but in this series the live music, enthusiasm of the kids and a special introduction of the Extreme Teen Bible will exemplify it is "cool" to Live God Loud. Ron's teaching will add a shot of encouragement to teens that will give them practical ideas on turning up the truth of God and His word, while turning down the lies of this world.

EZ Lesson Plan ISBN: 0-8499-8872-1 **Student's Guide ISBN: 0-8499-8873-X**

The Journey of Desire

John Eldredge

AVAILABLE JUNE 12, 2001

Desire can take on so many meanings in life. It can cause a marriage to fail, your job become meaningless and worst of all distort your faith. "Circumstances thwart our best laid plans," says John Eldredge, our acclaimed author of the book of the same title. The modern church mistakenly teaches people to kill desire and replace it with duty or obligation (calling in sanctification). As a result at best Christians tend to live safe, boring lives of resignation. At worst their desire eventually breaks out in destructive ways.

EZ Lesson Plan ISBN: 0-7852-9876-2 **Student's Guide ISBN: 0-7852-9877-0**

CONCLUSION LETTER

Dear friend,

I hope you have enjoyed this journey over the past four weeks. It has been my joy and privilege to be a part of your life.

My prayer is that these lessons have made a difference in your life.

Remember that you have unlimited potential and you can make a difference.

Never stop growing!

Your friend,

Todd Duncan
www.toddduncan.com

For more information about personal and professional growth
or to receive Todd's monthly e-newsletter "Life Wired"
visit www.theduncangroup.com or call 877-833-8633.

CLOSING NOTES

We hope you enjoyed your viewing of this powerful video. Let us review a few helpful reminders:

1. Review your notes carefully. Fill in any major points you remember, but failed to write down.
2. Make sure you have included all scripture references in your notes. Take time to study these in your personal time.
3. Ask questions and share you thoughts: If time and situation allows, ask questions still lingering in your mind. Also, now is a good time to share your personal thoughts on what you've heard and the impact its had on your own life … what you say may minister to someone else in the group.
4. Don't forget to pray: In your personal time, pray not only for your own clear understanding and insight, but pray for others in the group as well.

We're glad you joined us and pray this video has been an inspiration to your life.

If you enjoyed this video and want more information on other inspiring videos we publish, feel free to call us at 1-800-251-4000. We'll be glad to assist you.

Our blessing on you as you continue to grow in the love and power of our Lord and Savior, Jesus Christ.

